Giulio Mancini

D1297236

SAN DAMIANO
Recalling the Soul

Edizioni Porziuncola

San Damiano

Recalling the soul

This is a guide to the Spirituality of San Damiano.

It's not a guidebook for those who are in a hurry, but rather for those who have time, both to see the place and to discern its soul.

It's a question of "seeing and listening". Seeing the place – its poor walls - and listening to the stories recounted by the sources – the deeds which were done here through the Spirit and which burn like bright embers beneath the ashes.

San Damiano is a secret rendez-vous.

It requires sensitivity. As Paul Sabatier said, it is like a little "well of Sichem".

Blessed is the one who knows how to draw from it, "Sister Water, humble, precious and chaste".

An Encounter

One day in the autumn of 1205 the Lord was waiting here for Francis

On a morning in April of 1211 the Lord welcomed Clare together with her first sisters.

They were encounters and thus began their Christian adventure.

Brother, Sister. Perhaps here today the Lord will meet with you.

May your faith be firm and may the Lord grant you peace.

A Place of Peace

It's a simple place, not one crowded by the faithful and fine art.

Hidden on the slopes beneath Assisi in a charmingly naturalistic setting and intentionally sheltered from the flow of organized tourism, it is a call to the soul that brings one here.

Well over a thousand years old, yet all the same passed on to us through the restructuring that firstly Francis, then Clare and later the friars did here, it is a privileged place of the highest quality of evangelical spirituality, both the cradle and a reliquary of Franciscan origins.

God revealed himself here. The Spirit still makes its presence felt. From the shadows the faces of Francis and Clare appear; the Canticle of the Creatures oozes out from the walls.

These simple places speak in a silence which you can listen to. Here Francis' conversion to Christ and his radical response to that call took place. Here the love of Clare was consumed in living out the gospel as Mary had done. Both of them, through lives which were Christ-like, Marian, Church centred and very human - one almost another Christ the other almost another Mary – became evangelically speaking a restored House/Church in line with the command from the Crucifix.

This little God-space is reserved for Peace, the recovery of one's humanity, friendship with all creation but more than anything for that meeting with Someone who is waiting for you here.

May you listen carefully and enjoy a happy encounter.

San Damiano

The layout

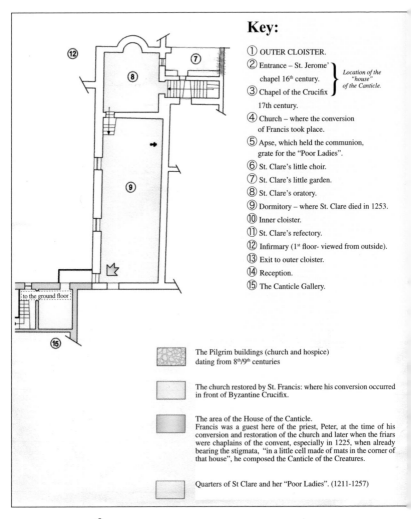

Key:

① OUTER CLOISTER.

② Entrance – St. Jerome' chapel 16th century.

③ Chapel of the Crucifix 17th century.

Location of the "house" of the Canticle.

④ Church – where the conversion of Francis took place.

⑤ Apse, which held the communion, grate for the "Poor Ladies".

⑥ St. Clare's little choir.

⑦ St. Clare's little garden.

⑧ St. Clare's oratory.

⑨ Dormitory – where St. Clare died in 1253.

⑩ Inner cloister.

⑪ St. Clare's refectory.

⑫ Infirmary (1st floor- viewed from outside).

⑬ Exit to outer cloister.

⑭ Reception.

⑮ The Canticle Gallery.

The Pilgrim buildings (church and hospice) dating from 8th/9th centuries

The church restored by St. Francis: where his conversion occurred in front of Byzantine Crucifix.

The area of the House of the Canticle.
Francis was a guest here of the priest, Peter, at the time of his conversion and restoration of the church and later when the friars were chaplains of the convent, especially in 1225, when already bearing the stigmata, "in a little cell made of mats in the corner of that house", he composed the Canticle of the Creatures.

Quarters of St Clare and her "Poor Ladies". (1211-1257)

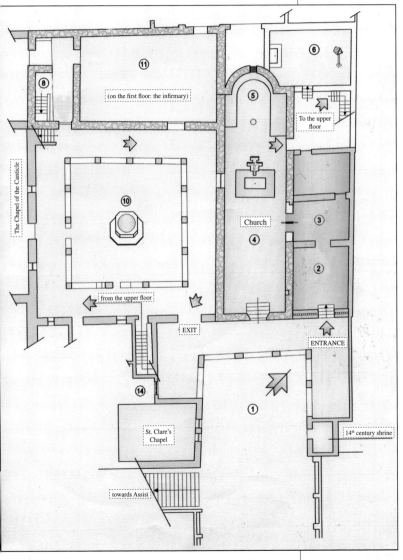

The Chapel of the Canticle

(on the first floor: the infirmary)

⑪

⑧

⑥

⑤

To the upper floor

⑩

Church ——

③

④

②

from the upper floor

EXIT

ENTRANCE

⑭

①

St. Clare's Chapel

14th century shrine

towards Assisi

Led by the Spirit,
he entered to pray in the little church of San Damiano.
The figure of Christ crucified spoke to him,
calling him by name:
"Francis, go rebuild my church." (2 Cel 593)

Praised be you, my Lord
with all your creatures
especially Brother Sun. (Canticle of the Creatures)

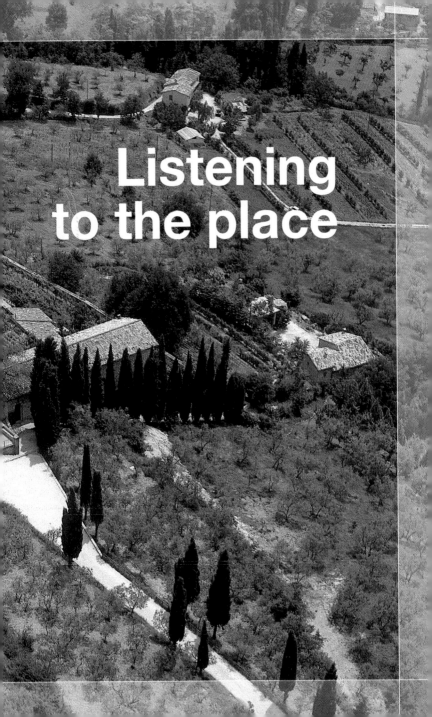

Listening
to the place

On the **Square outside**

We are in front of the Sanctuary: a place where God revealed Himself. Its only name throughout the centuries has been **San Damiano**, a doctor and martyr from Syria, whose cult – together with that of his brother Cosma – spread through the West in the fifth century.

The original church – dating back four or five centuries before St. Francis – is marked by the medieval restoration he himself completed. It went from Roman cemetery and rural Romanesque chapel, (9th/10th century) with hospice and priest's house (10th/12th century) to a convent for St. Clare with convent church and later a friary. (1211-1257)

Here in 1205, at the age of 24, Francis would feel himself called to conversion and the restoration of the church 📖1, where he stayed for some time as a guest of Father Peter, the priest.

In 1211 he brought the eighteen-year old Clare here who began the Order of the Poor Ladies (as Francis, imbued with the spirit of chivalry, called them). She would live out her love of Christ for 42 years here in poverty and joy in the manner of the Virgin Mary. Here in 1225, an infirm Francis, bearing the wounds of the stigmata, composed and sang the Canticle of the Creatures.

And here, on the 4th October 1226 the friars would bring his body to receive its last farewell from the Poor Ladies.

This little square welcomes you simply into its heart. In front of you stands the Sanctuary split into two parts.

On the left-hand side – above the porch with its low arches – is the humble façade with its off-centre rose-window. On the right-hand side – beyond the wooden doorway and below the part that has been added in poor stone – is the area where originally the priest's house and later the friars' quarters lay and also the area where the Canticle of the Creatures was composed.

Around it are the porches and buildings which were added between the fourteenth and eighteenth centuries. The poor rustic walls, which do seem to have been made of materials that were "begged for", highlight the local stone from which the church was constructed.

San Damiano.
Detail, fresco,
(14th cent.).

11

Votive frescoes (1510). *St. Clare, St. Francis, St. Sebastian* and *St. Roch*.

On the right, passing by several votive frescoes (1510) you come to a little bridge from where you can view the Garden of the Canticle. Then there is the Shrine of Majesty with fourteenth century fresco. It introduces the pictorial themes linking the Virgin Mary with the sanctuary. Mary is enthroned with Child, between St. Francis and St. Clare and within the arch, God the Father and Saints Damiano and Rufino (for the first time St. Francis and St. Clare are significantly placed on either side of the Madonna rather than Damiano and Rufino). At one's back lies the road from Assisi, a reminder of Francis' time when the links were by such hill roads to the Via Flaminia and the Via Francigena, well above the swampy plain.

Turning back towards the church it is not difficult to imagine Francis intent on bringing down the stones that he had begged in the town: *whoever gives me one stone will have a recompense, who two, two recompenses, who three, likewise.*

On the right-hand page: *Shrine of Majesty* (15th cent.). Below: *Garden of the Canticle and statue of St. Clare* by ROSIGNOLI.

Or when, transported by joy in the Spirit, he shouted from the wall to poor people who were passing: *Come and help me in this work... for Ladies whose holiness will give glory to their Heavenly Father throughout his church will come to live here.* Towards the left you will find the reception and access to information, guides and the booking of rooms for meetings. We may now enter. Not through the main door of the church however, but beyond it through the entrance on the right.

The **Chapels**

We are now in the **Chapel** of *St. Jerome*. In the semi-circular lunette in front of you, painted by **Tiberio d'Assisi** (1517) you will see the Madonna with Child between angels, St. Bernardine, St. Jerome, St. Francis and St. Clare. To your left you will find **St. Sebastian and St. Roch**, at the end of an interesting wall of Roman stone with the door which was once the entrance to the church.

This part - which used to be a single entity with the chapel next to it - is very important. Situated beside the church and separated from the convent, it was at first the priest's quarters. (A document from 1030 identifies a priest by the name of Runtum).

It was here that, in 1205, the young Francis - after having spent an entire month in hiding from his father in a secret cave nearby - was a guest of the old priest, Father Peter, at the very beginning of his conversion 📖3.

It was here that he lived out the drama of the break-up with his father 📖4, which culminated in his epic appearance before the bishop, Guido - where he gave back to his father even the clothes he was wearing. *From now on, I will no longer call Pietro di Bernardone, my father, but only Our Father who art in heaven.*

This place - once the convent of St. Clare was established in 1211 - then became the house of 3-4 friars, following upon the promise of Francis to Clare "to have for them particular attention and special care."

From that time, when Francis come to see Clare and her sisters he would stay here with the friars and share at their poor table. Once when Brother Angelo, "the king of verses" was present, *he (Francis) had hardly eaten four mouthfuls of bread, when he lifted his face towards heaven and remained there for a long time in total amazement.*

St. Sebastian and St. Roch. Details, fresco (1517).

Left, the painting of TIBERIO D'ASSISI, (1517).

Walled up old entrance.

15

Then recollecting himself, he shouted in a loud voice, "Praised be the Lord". And all of a sudden, he got up from the table and threw himself on the ground, immediately rapt in ecstasy. (The scene is delineated on the wall of the church immediately after the fourteenth-century frescoes of the "little window").

But above all it was here in the Winter of 1225/ Spring of 1226 that Francis – by now infirm, crucified with the stigmata, his sick eyes no longer being able to support the light of the sun or even fire and being tormented by rats in the place where he slept – stayed *for 50 days or more in a makeshift cell of mats in a corner of that house.* After a troubled yet exultant night, he rose in the morning to glorify his Lord who had assured him of his salvation, and he baptized the Italian common language by composing and singing the Praises of all creatures, the canticle of Brother Sun, the canticle of redeemed Creation and universal brotherhood.

It is indeed truly *in this place that the Canticle was born* 📖5.

In the next chapel (the Chapel of the Crucifix) – added in 1555 – hangs, wounded and suffering, the crucified Christ sculpted in wood by Brother Innocent of Palermo (1637).

It seems to exactly reflect the image of the crucified Christ whom St. Francis contemplated and wept over. How many people have cried over that face! Popular faith draws from it the sweetness of God's goodness. *I beg you, O Lord, may the sweet and ardent strength of your Love, enrapture my heart!*

The Confraternity of the Most Holy Crucifix take care of it.

Conforming to Christ – prayer

May the sweet and ardent strength of your love, Lord,
lift my mind from all things under heaven
so that I may die for love of your Love,
as you deigned to die
for love of my love.

(*St. Francis of Assisi*)

The **Church**

Now we are in the church; the heart of the sanctuary, the church of the conversion of St. Francis.

Constructed at different times, the oldest part is that at the bottom with its off-centre apse and sixteenth-century choir situated under the low vault.

The eye of faith shifts immediately to the **little wooden temple** of the tabernacle sitting on an **ancient column**: there is the Lord. Francis would say on bended knee: *We adore you, Lord Jesus Christ, here and in all your churches throughout the world and we bless you, because by your holy cross you have redeemed the world.*

It was the Sanctuary dedicated to San Damiano, on whose flank still lies the Pilgrim's Hospice. From 1150, with its Siro-byzantine icon of the Christ which spoke to Francis, it became –and still is today – the Sanctuary of the Crucifix.

The front part of the church, attached by the roughly ogival vault – on which the Dormitory of St. Clare rests – was a development for which perhaps Francis and Clare were responsible. Roman weight-bearing stones and natural projections of rock crop up at the entrance walls. Two **splayed windows**, on one side and the other, radiate light. A simple **decorative band** (13th cent.) gracefully divides it along the top.

At the top:
Tabernacle and old
Roman column.

Above:
Splayed window.

The church – outside of its two moments of community liturgy in the morning and in the evening – is reserved for silent prayer. In the peaceful half-light, the "signs" and the historical events which occurred here emerge, making it a living Franciscan memorial.

We too keep silence here. Looking at the walls, lovingly restored after the 1997 earthquake, we can try to "listen" to the life-giving secret of Francis and Clare.

19

It was here, still wandering restlessly in the crisis that marked the end of his worldly aspirations whether in commerce, civil, courtly, knightly or on the crusades, that Francis arrived as a supplicant in search of sense and illumination, carrying a prayer in his heart: *O Most High and glorious God, enlighten my heart!*

Here at the foot of the Crucifix, the Mercy of God which had been following him, reached into his heart, calling him by name: "*Francis!*"

He was immediately sent "*Go and rebuild my church that is in ruins!*". Trembling he replied, "*Yes, Lord, I will do it willingly.*" It was the grace of conversion. It was the grace of mission.

The idea came easily to him of taking from his father's draper's shop a load of precious cloth to sell in the market at Foligno, giving the proceeds to the priest. On the priest's refusal of it however, Francis made the great discovery that God did not want his money, but for him to personally labour with his hands. So he completed his last financial transaction on the little window of the church, discarding forever the merchant's purse. He will never touch it again, paying the consequences subsequently in his family, in society and in church life. He finds himself again, ejected from his former fatuous existence and marginalized by civil

St. Francis in prayer before the Crucifix. Detail, frescoes (1305-1315).

society, learning the ABC of the Gospel: the Christ who is Love, poor and crucified – conversion – son-like faith – prayer – persecution – humility – poverty – begging – manual work – leper houses – minority and joy.

Amongst the penniless friends who helped him in the restoration of the church of San Damiano, there was also, above all the presence of Father Peter. It was by being in his company that Francis learned to venerate those poor priests "who live according to the form of the Roman Church."

To these "facts" we now add the visible "signs" that bear witness to them.

On the right-hand wall, near the main entrance is "the window of the money". The frescoes which surround it by a local artist (1305-1315) depict Francis praying before the Crucifix; Francis, throwing the purse onto the window sill; Pietro di Bernardone (Francis' father) who is coming down angrily from Assisi (of which we are given an interesting view of the public buildings of the time). The scenes bring to mind the words of Jesus: Whoever loves his father or mother more than me is not worthy of me (Matt. 10,37).

Then beside a votive image of St Agnes Martyr, are the traces of that ecstasy of St. Francis to which we have already referred.

Above:
St. Agnes Martyr.
Detail, fresco
(13th cent.)

On the left:
Pietro di Bernardone coming down angrily from Assisi
(1305-1315).

21

**Prayer of St. Francis
in front of
the Crucifix.**

Most High and Glorious God
enlighten the dark places
of my heart.
Give me right faith, sure hope,
perfect charity,
profound humility, good sense
and understanding,
so that I may always
obey your holy and true
commandment. Amen.

We turn here to the sign above the altar, the sign of the Crucifix. It is a recent copy of the original Syrian-Byzantine icon of Sozio's Spoletan School (1150), now venerated in St. Clare's Basilica. It is a living Christ with eyes wide open, and body shining with light; it is the risen Christ who draws both angels and saints into the dance of life. It proclaims the dual theme – *God reigns from the wood* and *When I am lifted up from the earth I will draw all creatures to me* (Jn. 12,32).

It is the historical fount of the whole Franciscan movement throughout the centuries: There all are born. (Ps. 87,4). Foremost of all it is the archetypal image of the conversion and of the life of St. Francis. From his birth in the *He loved me and gave himself for me* (Galatians 2,20) to his life in the fashion of Christ poor and crucified; *For me to live is Christ* (Philippians 1,21) to the fullness *of I have been crucified with Christ* and in his appearance *as almost another Christ.*

The presence of the two saints on the side could suggest that the fresco predates Franciscanism: in the Franciscan period the images of St. Francis and St. Clare would have been preferred here in San Damiano as they were elsewhere.

To the back of the apse, there is another sign: a majestic Roman-Byzantine **Madonna Odighitria** (Madonna who indicates the way) with raised crown and halo, who indicates the Child in her arms as the Way to follow. On one side is San Damiano, who gives his name to this church, and on the other St.Rufino first bishop of Assisi, indicating that this church belonged to the bishop. Taking account of the fact that the Poor Ladies' choir would have been located behind the apse, the Odighitria represents the gospel and Marian Form of Life which Francis wrote for Clare between 1211-13; to live the Gospel in the manner of Mary, as *another Mary*. A life that is inspired by the Trinitarian relationships of the Virgin and her gospel perfection: as *Daughter and Handmaid of the Father, Bride of the Holy Spirit*, in the perfection of the Holy Gospel.

Nuns' Grate.

There is yet another sign under the Odighitria: between the cornice and the two painted candlesticks, one can see over the top of the choir, an opening in the wall. It was the place where the **Grate** (now amongst the

relics conserved in St. Clare's Basilica) was situated; the place where the Word of God was heard and Communion with the Body and Blood of Christ was made.

In front of, and through this grate, Francis and the other friars used to provide the Poor Ladies the spiritual sustenance of the Word of God. It was here that he gave his famous sermon of the ashes. When the sisters were gathered together in the choir, Francis remained for a long time in silence, his eyes raised to heaven. Then – like a prophet who spoke more by his actions than his words – he asked that they bring him ashes. He made a circle with them on the ground around him and then spread them over his head. All at once he rose and intoned the Psalm *Miserere*. Then he left hurriedly, leaving them astounded. He was simply ashes, the Fire was Jesus Christ.

But the substantial food that was administered at the grating was the Most Holy Body of Jesus Christ. Not for nothing beside the wall is there a **little niche**, under which is written in gothic script "Hic locus corporis"

Through this grate the last act of Francis on this earth was played out. His body, bearing the stigmata, was shown to the Poor Ladies, on the morning of 4 October 1226. The grate was unhinged and Clare and her sisters could have their Father amongst them for their veneration and mourning: *the Father that no longer speaks to them, and will not return again* 📖6.

At the top: *Niche*; in the middle: *the Eternal Father*; bottom: *death of St. Clare*. Details, fresco (16th cent.).

Finally a mention for the precious inscription which surrounds the top of the choir and bears witness with the following words in Latin. *Non vox sed votum, non clamor sed amor, non cordula sed cor psallit in aure Dei.* They speak of the essence of the prayerful and loving experience which was lived out here: not voice but soul, not words but love, not instruments but the heart prays in the ear of God. *The voice chimes together with the heart, and the heart with God.*

Well up above the altar some **sixteenth-century frescoes** have re-emerged: local stories about St. Clare which echo those of St. Francis at the entrance.

St. Clare's Little Choir

We pass on to the areas of the Convent of "Our Lady of San Damiano", where Clare and the Poor Ladies lived from 1211 to 1253/1257: the **Choir** – the little **Garden** – the **Oratory** – the **Dormitory** – the **Cloister** – the **Infirmary** – the **Refectory**.

In this little place, the virgin Clare enclosed herself for love of her Heavenly Spouse. For 42 years she broke the alabaster of her body in order to fill the Church with a sweet-smelling fragrance.

The form of their life was *to follow the footsteps of Christ and his most Holy Mother, enclosed corporally and in unity of spirit, to serve the Lord in the most high poverty, dedicated freely to Him.*

This is the place where Lady Clare, precious and adamantine stone, became the foundation stone for all the others. Noble born, but more noble by virtue of grace, physically a virgin and most pure in spirit... constant in her decisions, ardent and enthusiastic in her love of God, full of wisdom and humility: her name meant clarity, her life demonstrated it even more, her light shone most clearly through her virtue.

We cross a little hallway which introduces us to those places where the poverty is palpable.

On the left hand side of the burial ground: local travertine stone delineating an ancient circular entrance behind which an ancient Roman stone tomb was found.

It was called the **burial ground**. The cloistered sisters who died within these walls were buried here. In 1257 their remains were removed to the convent of St. Clare in the town of Assisi. They included Blessed Ortolana, mother of St. Clare (1238), St. Agnes, sister of Clare (1253), Blessed Amata, Sister Andrea (1254), and Sister Illuminata.

From the gothic entrance you can admire the **Little Choir of St. Clare**. It's only a part of the old choir, shortened in 1482 by the wall on which Mezastris painted the fresco of the **Crucifix**. But even with this limitation, what an impression the choir makes! On the right – under the stained glass window of P. Bracaloni – the original wooden furnishings speak to us with an austere but sweet voice.

P. Bracaloni,
*Stained Glass
Window.*

The back-rests and the little roughly hewn wooden seats of oak, with the dossal in front and the lecterns at either side, all worn away by time, are moving relics. One can imagine the figures of the Poor Ladies here, vigilant both night and day at the feet of their Lord, like Mary of Bethany, for the only thing really necessary (Luke: 10, 42) with their lights lit awaiting the arrival of the Bridegroom like the wise virgins (Matt. 25, 1-13).

It is the heart of the convent. It tells us how prayer took the place of honour here, praise, listening, intercessions, contemplation and the expectance of the Bridegroom. Here at midnight, Lady Clare, was first here to light the lights, prepare the psalters and breviaries in order to favour the ardour of the soul.

The Sisters celebrated the Divine Office according to the usage of the Friars Minor, and could therefore have breviaries, reading them without singing.

It was here that the mystic events of Clare's charismatic life occurred. Like the vision of the infant child during the preaching of a sermon by Brother Filippo d'Atri: *where two or three are gathered together in my*

St. Clares's
wooden choir.

name, I am in the midst of them (Matt. 18, 20).

Or as when the vision of the splendour of the stars and red fire encircled Clare's head, or when on returning from prayer, when, *the Sisters rejoiced as if she had come directly from heaven.*

It was inside here, in her interior union with her Lord and Spouse, that the flame of Clare's love overflowed in its feminine fashion in the four letters sent to Agnes of Prague (1235- 1253).

On the **wooden lectern** transcribed on parchment are the **names** of some fifty sisters, who are identified as such on an official document of 8th June 1238. Reading their names makes them appear as still present.

It is not for nothing that the daughters of Clare spread all over the world (18,000 in 800 convents) come together here spiritually to the focal centre of their hidden lives, wishing to enflame their prayers through that of their Mother, called by the Church to bear witness to God's mercy and peace.

Now, by means of an old and somewhat inconvenient staircase, we ascend to the upper floor.

P. Mezastris,
Crucifixion.
Fresco 1482.

*Burial Ground
and old stairwell*
of the Convent.

29

The **Little Garden**

It's a very small roof-garden, at the end of a small courtyard between two outer walls; a little flower-bed suspended above the Spoletan valley which spreads out below your feet.

It is said that Clare grew roses and violets here, and cultivated her songs of charity and humility. A disciple of the Canticle of the Creatures composed by Francis, and which she had heard from him, (reminders of the Canticle are to be found engraved on the memorial stone and on Rosignoli's bronze relief) made her love to be here to contemplate God's wonders.

She used to say to the sisters: *When you see beautiful trees, leaved and in flower, you should praise God.* And similarly, *When you see men and other creatures, you should always, of all things and in all things, praise God*

The stairwell of the convent and St. Clare's *little garden.*

31

St. Clare's Oratory

Between the dormitory and the infirmary and above the choir of the church, we find this intimate part of the convent, embellished with **fourteenth-century frescoes**, of particular relevance to the historical events which occurred here.

It was in this place that Clare kept the Eucharist, where she remained in prolonged prayer during her long illnesses and where with the sign of the cross she healed the sick. Two signs attract the attention.

The first is the **Ciborium** on the left hand side, hollowed into the wall and surrounded by frescoes. In front of it is Clare, leading the ranks of sisters kneeling in prayer. Inside,

Ciborium in wall, (14th cent.).

33

St. Clare
and the nuns
in prayer in front of
the ciborium.
Detail, fresco
(14th cent.).

St. Francis,
Madonna and Child
and St. Clare.
Details, fresco
(14th cent.).

at the back is the figure of the Child Jesus, standing upon the Eucharistic casket. They remind us of the two dramatic moments when the Saracens of Frederick II besieged the convent in 1240, and later when the town itself was besieged in 1241 both attacks repulsed through the power of prayer.

In both of these cases, Clare the meek contemplative, reacted with the innate pride of her noble race, united with humble and confident prayer before the most holy body of her Lord. *Do not be afraid* – she said to her sisters, terrified by the Saracens who were already breaking into the cloister – *I will make a shield for you.* Prostrating herself, she turned towards the Lord: *Protect your servants from these wild beasts for I am not capable of defending them.* They heard a voice like that of a Child reply: *I will always protect you.*

As for the town, on the point of surrender, she gathered her sisters together here to fast and cover their heads with ashes. *Save this town which belongs to you and which for your love sustains us.* The following morning, *that army left, crushed and broken.*

Assisi still remembers this liberation and in gratitude to its sweet and proud daughter holds the annual *Feast of the Vow* every 22nd June.

The other sign is in the little **apse**, behind the old altar. The arch is framed by five discs with the **four evangelists** and in the centre, the **etimasía- throne**, of the Lord who will come. From the basin three figures appear, **Virgin with Child** in swaddling cloths, and the saints, **Francis and Clare**.

Four discs with
The Evangelists and –
at the centre – that
of *The Lord's throne*.
Detail, fresco
(14th cent.).

It bears witness to the Marian nature of the Oratory. It was consecrated, we are told, by Umbrian bishops who proclaimed with Francis the Indulgence of Forgiveness at the Porziuncola in 1216, and bore the name Our Lady of San Damiano: a significant repetition of Our Lady of the Porziuncola, which bound together Francis and Clare. It was in the latter church that Francis had tonsured Clare, the evening after Palm Sunday in 1211.

But the three images also exalt the *material conformity* of Francis and Clare, beside the Mother of Our Lord, "perfection of the Holy Gospel.".

Outside, rising up over the right-hand wall and towering above the roof-line lies the *Open Bell tower*, which gives San Damiano its characteristic profile in the surrounding view.

San Damiano's
Bell-tower.

St. Clare's Dormitory

Entrance to
St. Clare's *Dormitory.*

We reach the dormitory via three worn-down steps. We are over the vault of the Church below. It strikes one as a bare and austere space, which is illuminated only by the two windows which overlook the cloister below. Here the sisters and Clare herself, took some brief repose, lined up together on straw mattresses, suffering the biting cold of winter and the suffocating heat of summer. The fourteenth century Crucifix reigns over the room where Lady Poverty is Queen.

It was here Clare used to encourage her Sisters to rise at midnight to praise God.

It was here Clare bore with joyful love her illness: embroidering linen and silk for poor churches. Occasionally she would be rapt up in mystical experiences, which established her in communion with the Passion of the Lord.

It was here that she experienced the ecstasy of her last Christmas (1252). Having been left on her own by the Sisters for night prayer, by a remarkable miracle she was able to see the holy rites being celebrated in the church of St. Francis in Assisi 📖7. It was an audio-visual experience before the arrival of the technology of today, for which Clare was declared Patron Saint of Television (1958).

Here after 1243, she lived – in order to consign her charismatic heritage to the Church – the long torment of the drafting and the approval of *the Rule* as she explains in her *Testament.*

Visited twice in the last days of her life by Pope Innocent IV, Clare related to him her burning desire *to have the Order's Rule officially approved in a papal bull: so that one day she may place it to her mouth and then, the following day die. And as she had wanted, so it happened.* The Pope finally signed the document on 9th August 1253. On the 10th it was brought to her: she clasped it to her breast, kissing it both on one side and the other 📖8.

And it was here again towards evening on 11th August, celebrating an intense liturgy for the commendation of her soul – "commendatio animae" that Clare died, some 27 years after Francis.

A vision of heavenly virgins, led by the Mother of God approached her bed in a courtly procession to cover her with a golden veil and to present her to the King of Glory.

Her last words were perhaps the most exquisite of all the lives of the saints. They surpass even those of Francis who had nonetheless "welcomed death singing". *Go in peace* – she murmured – *my blessed soul. He who created you loves you like a mother loves her little son.* A moment later she added: *And you, Lord, be blessed because you created me.* She thus completed her Passover, her *transitus*. "Blessed was her departure from this valley of tears. Blessed her arrival into the celestial life" (From the liturgy of the Poor Clares).

A Sister, giving evidence at the Canonization hearing, declared: *Lady Clare passed from this life to the Lord, truly pure and without stain, without the darkness of sin to the brightness of the eternal light.*

At the end of the room on the right, on the way out, we pass over **the original steps**, uncovered in the 1993 restoration, which at the time of St. Clare, descended to the Dormitory's drawbridge: let down to the cloister at dawn and raised up once again in the evening.

Crucifix,
by unknown Author,
(14th cent.).

The Canticle Gallery

From the balcony which overhangs the flower-covered cloister, flanked on the northern side by Mount Subasio, one crosses a little hall. On the left, if you are interested in art, you can go into the **Canticle Gallery**.

Recently moved here from the ground floor, its aim is to keep alive the Christological and cosmic inspiration of Francis' Canticle of the Creatures. Through selected art exhibitions artists-friends interpret for us today its message of beauty, humanity and fraternity. Small works of art, prints and originals are on show for the pilgrim visitors to the Sanctuary.

The Canticle Gallery has housed throughout the years the most diverse types of artistic expression: from graphics to musical compositions, from ceramics to paintings, from icons to sculpture.

Below:
Our Lady's chapel, a multifunctional room sited under the square in front of the Sanctuary.

On the left:
Mother Earth.
Work by
GIUSTINA DE TONI.

41

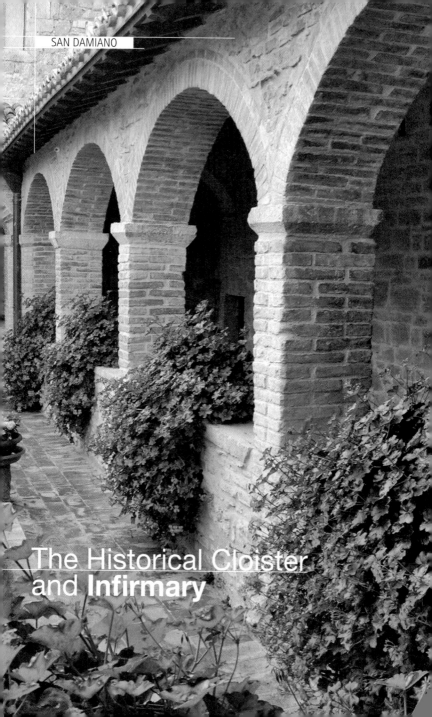

The Historical Cloister
and **Infirmary**

*The Infirmary
of the Friary
(15th cent.).*

The structure of the cloister, already in being at the time of the St. Clare, was completed between the fifteenth and eighteenth centuries. The saint was discomfited by the collapse of the main door to the cloister and lifting it up from the ground, just as if it had been a cloak, required the friars' help.

The two pre-Franciscan structures meet here in a corner, which is decorated on the lower level by two **frescoes** of Eusebio Perugino (1507): the Annuciation and St. Francis receiving the stigmata.

In front, in local travertine stone, is the compact Romanesque structure of the **Pilgrim's Hospice** (10th century). The ground floor was then used as St. Clare's refectory. The upper floor being transformed into a dormitory for sisters who were ill.

The Infirmary, as it came to be known, is now part of the friary. An austere environment, still maintained in its original state by strong roof trusses, then divided internally into ten fifteenth century cells, corresponding to the windows seen from outside, it is full of evocative reminders of Clare: *The blessed Mother Clare had*

*Cloister
(15th-18th cent.).*

43

Cloister
(15th-18th cent.).

Eusebio Perugino,
Annunciation. Detail,
fresco (1507)..

compassion for the sick: whilst she was well herself, she served them, washed their feet, gave them water for their hands and washed their seats.

On the right side, is the wall of the church, on which traces of St. Francis' restoration work still perhaps remain. It was in this vicinity that, in September 1240, Saracen mercenaries pressed menacingly upon "the virgins' cloister". It was near the exit of the Refectory that Clare, infirm and supported by two sisters, confronted them holding the body of Christ in front of her, contained in its ivory and silver casket.

Eusebio Perugino,
The stigmata
of St. *Francis.*
Detail, fresco (1507).

It was here also that three months after her death, that the Saint's canonization process was held. Presided over by Bishop Bartolomeo of Spoleto (Friars Leone, Angelo, and the chaplain Marco) from 24th to 28th November 1253, the tribunal collected under oath the personal and communal evidence of the Poor Ladies: precious and enchanting texts which have come down in the Umbrian popular dialect to our times.

The conclusion is surprising: *They said with one mind: Never, since the Virgin Mary on, has there been a holier woman than the aforesaid Saint Clare.*

45

St. Clare's Refectory

St. Clare's refectory.
On the back walls
two seventeenth
century
frescoes from the
SERMEI school.

This is the place where the Poor Ladies ate and met together, with its **original wooden furnishings**. Flowers on the table mark where Clare originally sat.

The double cross vault on low pillars (originally the ceiling was framed with beams) makes it the finest place in the convent, the walls at either end being decorated by two **seventeenth-century frescoes**, the work of pupils of Sermei (1619).

Many events occurred here.

As far as the table was concerned they did not occupy themselves with it overmuch. *The robust and healthy among us* – Clare wrote to Agnes of Prague in 1238 – *fast every day with Lenten foods, apart from Sunday. Fasting does not apply to sisters who are ill.*

This meant generally, bread and water. She was particularly happy to accept the pieces of bread begged by the friars: happier with these pieces than entire loaves.

In this too *she exhorted the sisters to conform themselves, in their poor little nest, to the Poor Christ.*

This Holy Poverty, when necessary, also made for miracles!

The miracle of the olive oil, an empty vase found filled through Providence on the little wall near the exit, where it had been left for Brother Bentivenga, the friar who was responsible for procuring it. He murmured *These ladies have called me to make fun of me.*

The miracle of the fifty slices of bread, when the convent had only one loaf and the half of it had already been given to the friars.

The miracle of the loaves marked with the sign of the cross, when Clare blessed them on the insistence of their guest Pope Gregory IX.

The refectory was also the meeting point. The chapters of the community were held here *once a week:* a Chapter of the Faults which were humbly confessed and a Chapter to discuss *those things which were of use and common benefit to the Convent, with the aim of maintaining the unity of charity practised amongst them and the peace.*

Here also Clare welcomed Cardinals and Popes when they wished to meet her. There is the famous episode which occurred in July 1228, when after the canonization of St. Francis Pope Gregory came here. Moved by their *High Povert*y, he wanted to induce them to accept some earthly possessions. He heard the reply: *Under no circumstances and never for all eternity do I wish to be dispensed from following the Poor Christ.* Clare was referring to the "Privilege" of Holy Poverty" which she had already obtained from Pope Innocent III in 1216. She had this confirmed by Pope Gregory IX, in the same year, 1228.

It is possibly opportune to say here that under the old flooring, towards the centre, and several metres below floor level, a cave is to be found – now somewhat extended. In its primitive state it would have been the cave in which the young Francis hid himself for a full month to escape his father's wrath.

St. Clare's *refectory.*

St. Agnes' Oratory

Going out you can ask to see – when it is possible – an old place which the friars call the *Focone* or the **Common Hearth**: as well as the little stained glass window that gives a little view of the internal cloister with **St. Clare's Well**. Those in the Convent concerned with the domestic tasks must have met at this common hearth. From the 1600s however the Friars would have warmed themselves here prior to their nightly repose.

One can reach a private chapel, made up of two of the Infirmary cells, by means of a steep little staircase which follows on the right of the barrel-vaulted walkway – but it is reserved solely for those who wish to remain in prolonged silent prayer and adoration. It bears the name of St. Agnes, St. Clare's sister, who died in San Damiano in November 1253.

The Word of the Lord echoes here: *Come away to a solitary place, and rest here a while* (Mark 6,31).

The Common Hearth. Below and to the left, St. Clare's Well.

St. Agnes, Contemporary work.

Francis go...

From the time that Francis began here aged 24, and Clare aged 18, San Damiano has been a free gift for everyone, but above all for young people. It has a simple beauty, which speaks meekly in *spirit and in truth*.

I hope that you may have sensed it, that you may have caught the aroma of the Gospel: the Words by which the Spirit reached Francis and Clare. Words that were lived and shown to be true here.

The Lord knows you by your name. God has pronounced it here.

Now it is time to leave: *Go* .... You too can try to do something: Heal yourself, rebuild that old poor self which has been left alone, with its wishes and its dreams.

If you want you can find here a listening ear and an opportunity also to meet with a friar.

Goodbye, brother! Goodbye sister!

May the Lord grant you peace.

May He always be with you.

And may he contrive it so that you are always with Him!

Outside there is the road which Francis walked back up, different from the way he had come down. Don't go away hurriedly. The valley spreads out below you. The hills come to meet you. "Everything sings and shouts with joy!" (Ps. 64,16), the creation throbs with God.

It is the time to attune your heart to Francis' canticle:

*Praise and bless my Lord
and thank and serve Him,
with profound humility!*

Matthew 19,21
*Fixing him, he
loved him
and said to him,
"One thing alone
you lack,
Go, sell all
you have…
And then come
and follow me".*

Matthew 16,25
*Whoever seeks to
save his own life
will lose it,
But whoever loses
his own life
for my sake
will find it.*

Luke 10,21
*You have hidden
these things from
the wise and
learned.*

Spiritus meus attenuabitur dies mei breui-
abuntur. ¶ Solum mihi superest sepulcri.
Non peccaui. ¶ In amaritudinibus moratur
oculus meus. libera me domine ¬ pone me
iuxta te ¬ cuiuslibet manus pugnet me. dies
mei transierunt cogitaciones mee dissipate sunt
torquentes cor meum. ¶ Noctem uerterunt
in diem ¬ rursum post tenebras spero lucem. Si
sustinuero infernus domus mea est ¬ in tenebris straui lectulum meum. Putredi-
ni dixi pater meus es. mater mea ¬ soror
mea uermibus. Vbi est ergo nunc presto-
latio mea ¬ pacienciam meam tu es domine
deus meus.

Peccantem me cotidie ¬ non me pe-
nitentem timor mortis conturbat me. qui-
a in inferno nulla est redemptio. miserere
mei deus ¬ salua me. ¶ Deus in noie...

Quo salutem me fac ¬ in nomine tuo libera me. Qui-
a pelli mee consumptis carnibus adhesit os meum ¬ derelicta sunt tantummodo
labia circa dentes meos. Miseremini mei
miseremini mei saltem uos amici mei. quia
manus domini tetigit me. Quare persequimi-
ni me sicut deus. ¬ carnibus meis saturami-
ni. Quis mihi tribuat ut scribantur ser-
mones mei. Quis mihi det ut exarentur
in libro stilo ferreo ¬ plumbi lamina. Uel certe
sculpantur in silice. Scio enim quod redemp-
tor meus uiuit. et in nouissimo die de terra
surrecturus sum. et rursum circumdabor pel-
le mea. ¬ in carne mea uidebo deum saluatorem

meum. Quem uisurus sum ego
et oculi mei conspecturi sunt ¬ non al-
ta est hec spes mea in sinu...

Domine secundum actum meum noli...

nichil dignum in conspectu tuo...

deprecor maiestatem tuam...

dolens iniquitatem meam...

lava me domine ab iniusticia...

Preliato meo munita me...
...sunt dies iusticie ecclesie me-
...terer. Fuisses es... non eram.
clarus ad nihilum... ¬ tanquam
tus dies meos. Sinuerterer breuis
ergo ut plangam paululum do-
lorem meum quam uadam ¬ non reuertar
nebulam ¬ operiam mortis caligine
miserie ¬ tenebris. ubi umbra
mullus ordo. si sempiternus error
tensi. ¬ stud... ¬ solempni
post festum omnium sanctorum
tium. libera me domine...
¶ instanti...

Libera me domine de uiis inferni...

Listen to the Sources

...he remained vigilant to welcome secretly the sources of the divine murmuring.

He was by now a totally changed man, both in his mind and also soon to be in his heart, when one day he passed by the church of San Damiano, almost in ruins and deserted by everyone. Led by the Spirit he went in to pray. He humbly prostrated himself devotedly before the Crucifix, and touched in an extraordinary way by divine grace, he found himself completely changed. Whilst he was thus profoundly moved, all of a sudden, the painted image of the crucified Christ spoke to him: "Francis - he said, calling him by name – go and rebuild my house which as you see is all in ruins". Francis, trembling and full of wonder almost lost control of his senses at these words. But immediately he set himself to obey and concentrated everything on fulfilling this invitation.

From that time he could no longer hold back the tears and cried aloud about the Passion of Christ, which was always before his eyes. *(2nd Life of Thomas of Celano)*

 1

The vocation

 2

The restoration of San Damiano

Upon returning to the church of San Damiano, fervent and full of happiness, he made for himself a hermit's habit and comforted the priest of that church using the same words with which the bishop had comforted him. Thus, going back into the town, he began to cross the streets and squares, infused with the Spirit, giving praise to the Lord. On finishing these praises, he set himself to obtaining the necessary materials for the restoration of the church. He would say: "Whoever gives me one stone will have a recompense; whoever two stones, two recompenses; whoever three, the same number of recompenses!"

How much he suffered in this rebuilding process, it would take a long time and be difficult to explain. Used to an easy life in his father's house, here he was carrying stones upon his back, and enduring many tribulations in order to serve God.

That good priest looked kindly upon Francis throwing himself fully into a work that perhaps went beyond his capacities. Moved by the sight, and despite his own poverty, he sought to prepare him a special meal knowing that in his home he had been used to many comforts.

One day Francis noticed the special attention that the priest was giving him, and thought to himself. "Do you think will find a priest like this everywhere who will surround you with fine things? This is not the life of a poor man that you have embraced. As the beggar goes from door to door cup in hand, you too must do likewise, for the love of Christ". *(Legend of the Three Companions)*

Money like dust

Joyful because of the vision and the words of the Crucifix, Francis got up, made the sign of the cross, and mounting his horse went to the town of Foligno carrying with him a load of various coloured cloths. There he sold both horse and merchandise and returned immediately back to San Damiano.

He found the priest again, and after having reverently kissed his hands with faith and devotion he gave him the money, begging the priest that he might be allowed to come live with him. The priest finally gave in to the second request but, for fear of Francis' relatives, he would not accept the money. So Francis, truly despising wealth, threw the money upon a window sill, as if it were no more than a handful of dust. *(Legend of the Three Companions)*

Persecution by his father

Whilst he was prolonging his stay there, his worried father began to go searching to see what had become of his son. He came to know that he had become completely changed and was living at San Damiano and sought to find him.

Francis had by now become one of Christ's knights, when he learned that his family was threatening him. He sought to hide from his father's wrath, by taking refuge in a secret cave and hiding himself there for an entire month. The cavern was known to only one member of the family who used to take food to him there, which the young man consumed without letting himself be seen.

Until one day, fired up with enthusiasm, he left the cave and gaily set off walking towards Assisi at a lively pace.

On seeing him at first, those who knew him as he was

before began to insult him, shouting that he was mad and had lost his senses and throwing stones and mud at him.

The news of what was happening spread throughout the squares and streets of the town, until it came also to the ears of his father. Hearing how he was being maltreated, he went out immediately to take charge of him. Beside himself with rage, he hurled himself upon him as a wolf upon a sheep, grabbing him and bringing him back to his house. Here he locked him up in a small dark room for several days.

Francis would not let himself be moved neither by threats, chains or blows. Only it happened that his father had to leave the house for an urgent business matter, and accordingly the prisoner was left alone with his mother. She did not approve of her husband's methods, and spoke only kindly words to her son, not succeeding however in turning him away from his intention. Overborne by maternal love, one day she loosed the chains and allowed him to go free.

Francis gave thanks to God Almighty, and returned to San Damiano. *(Legend of the Three Companions)*

 5

The *Canticle of the Creatures* is born

T wo years before he died, when he was already gravely ill and above all suffering greatly with his eyes, he came to stay at San Damiano in a little cell made of mats... The weather at that time was very cold.

Francis stayed at San Damiano for over 50 days. He wasn't able to stand natural light during the day or the brightness of fire at night, and remained always in the darkness of his cell or the building. On top of that however, he also suffered atrocious pain in his eyes, both night and day so that he could hardly rest nor sleep, and the pain of this together with his other infirmities was increasing and getting worse.

As if that was not enough, if he wished on occasion to rest or sleep, the building and little cell where he lay (it was made of mats and sited in the corner of the building) was so infested with rodents who jumped over and ran around him that he found it impossible to sleep. The animals disturbed

him even in his prayers. They tormented him not only at night but also even during the day, even whilst he was eating they would jump up onto the table. Both he and his companions thought that it was to tempt him.

One night whilst he was dwelling upon these tribulations, he began to feel self-pity and prayed within himself, "Lord, come to help me in my infirmities so that I may be able to bear them patiently".

And immediately he received the message in spirit, "Brother, be happy and exult in your infirmities and tribulations; from now on you will live in complete serenity, as if you were already in my Kingdom".

Rising in the morning, he said to his companions, "I want to compose a new *Praise to the Lord through creation,* to praise Him, for my consolation and for my neighbour's edification. Every day we use these creatures and without them we cannot live, and we often offend our Creator by means of them. Every day we show ourselves to be ungrateful for these great benefits, and we don't give praise for them as we should, to our Creator and Giver of every good thing".

And sitting down he concentrated himself on reflecting, then he said, *"Most High, almighty good Lord..."*. Francis also composed the tune and taught it to his companions.

His spirit was immersed in such great sweetness and consolation that he wanted to send for Brother Pacifico – at that time known as the "king of the verses" and who was a very kind singing master – and to assign to him several able and spiritual brothers so that they might go throughout the world preaching and praising God. He wanted one of them who was capable of preaching, to address the people with a sermon, and on finishing this all together would sing the Praises of God. When the Praises were finished, the preacher would say to the people, "We are minstrels of the Lord and the return which we want from you for this is this: that you may live in true penitence". *(Legend of Perugia)*

His friars and spiritual children ran together with the crowds from the neighbouring towns to have the joy themselves of participating in the solemn funeral rites, and passed the whole of the night in which Francis died praying and singing psalms.

At dawn the following day the townspeople of Assisi arrived with the clergy and taking the holy body they transported it with honour through the town amidst hymns, songs and trumpet blasts. Everyone, furnished with branches of olive, or of other trees formed the procession singing at the top of their voices praises and prayers to the Lord, among the splendour of innumerable candles.

When they came to the place where Francis had founded the Order of holy virgins and Poor Ladies, to the church of San Damiano, where his favourite daughters who he had won for the Lord lived, they laid his holy body down. The grate, through which the handmaids of Christ received communion was opened, as was the coffin... and behold, Lady Clare, who was truly radiant through her wealth of virtues, the first mother amongst all of them because she had been his little plant, came with her children to see the Father who no longer spoke with them and would no longer come back to them because he was going elsewhere.

And looking upon him, crying and groaning with heart-broken voices they expressed their trembling and devoted grief. *(1ˢᵗ Life of Thomas of Celano)*

 6

The Poor Ladies' weeping

As she in his illness remembered her Christ, so also Christ visited her in her sickness.

At the time on Christmas day, when the world rejoices with the angels for the Child that is newly born, all the Ladies went to say matins in the choir, leaving their Mother weighed down with her illness. She began to think of the little child Jesus and was pained not to be able to join in singing his praises, sighing, she said to Him, "Lord God, here I am left alone for You!". And behold, all of a sudden she

 7

The last Christmas

began to hear resounding in her ears the marvellous concert that was taking place in the church of St. Francis.

She heard the friars singing their psalms full of joy; she followed the harmonies of the singers and could enjoy the sound of the instruments. The place was not in fact close enough to allow the human perception of those sounds: either the celebration was rendered divinely sonorous in order to reach her, or else her hearing was enhanced beyond human limits.

What surpassed this marvellous hearing however was the fact that she could even see the Lord's crib.

(Legend of St. Clare)

 8

The privilege of poverty

The aforesaid lady and holy Mother being now close to death, one night after the Sabbath, began to speak in these words: *"Go safely in peace, because you will have a good escort; for He who created you first sanctified you and then created you and put the Holy Spirit inside you and He has always looked upon you as a mother who looks upon her little child that she loves."* And she added, *" May you be blessed oh Lord, You who created me".* She then said many things regarding the Trinity, but so softly that the Sisters could not hear them well.

One sister asked her with whom or to whom she spoke. To this she replied, *"I am speaking to my soul".*

At the end of her life, having called all her Sisters to her, she recommended most carefully to them the Privilege of poverty. She greatly wished to have the Order's Rule approved and sealed, so that she might be able to kiss that seal on one day and on the next day die; and as she wished so it happened. A friar came with the sealed parchments, which she reverently took, even though she was near to death, and placed the seal to her mouth in order to kiss it. The following day Lady Clare passed from this life, one who was truly transparent and without stain or the darkness of sin, to the brightness of that eternal light.

(Legend of St. Clare)

The Canticle of the Creatures

Most High, almighty and good Lord, to you alone are praise, glory, honour and every blessing.
To you alone they belong and no-one is worthy to speak your name Praised be you, my Lord, with all your creatures especially for Brother Sun who gives us day and through him you enlighten us.
He is beautiful and radiant with great splendour, and a symbol of you, Most High.
Praised be you, my Lord, for Sister Moon and the stars which pure, precious and beautiful you created in heaven.
Praised be you, my Lord, for Brother Wind for breezes, clouds, and every type of weather good or bad, for through them you provide nourishment to your creatures.
Praised be you, my Lord, for Sister Water, who is most useful, humble, precious and chaste.
Praised be you, my Lord, for Brother Fire, by whom you provide light at night and he is fine, joyful, strong and robust.
Praised be you, my Lord, for our Sister Mother Earth, who gives us sustenance and governs us and produces various fruits and colourful flowers and herbs.
Praised be you, my Lord, for those who forgive for love of you and suffer infirmity and tribulation.
Blessed are those who endure these with a peaceful spirit, for by you, Most High, will they be crowned.
Praised be you, My Lord, for our Sister Bodily Death, from which no living being can escape: woe to those who die in mortal sin; blessed those who you find doing your most holy will, for the second death will do them no harm.
Praise and bless my Lord and give thanks to Him and serve him with great humility.

63

Indice

© 2009 Edizioni Porziuncola
Via Protomartiri Francescani, 2
06088 Santa Maria degli Angeli -
Assisi (PG)
www.edizioniporziuncola.it

ISBN 978-88-270-0633-7

Cover Photograph
Mauro Gottardo

Photograph
Mauro Gottardo, Massimo Lelli
and Edizioni Porziuncola Archives

Translation from Italian
Br. Eunan McMullan ofm

Printed and arranged by
Studio VD
Città di Castello (PG)
studio.vd@virgilio.it

San Damiano: amongst the most
important and authentic
sanctuaries of Franciscanism.
It is the site of the vocation of Francis
of Assisi, where he composed the
"Canticle of the Creatures"
and the first convent of the Poor Clares,
where St. Clare lived until her death.

ISBN 978-88-270-0

9 788827 006

€ 5,00

Edizioni Porziuncola